"A compassionate, honest, and in..
both to those who have faced div..
it. Jenny's personal journey will inspire others to start their own,
finding the true peace, healing and restoration that only come from
God." – Lexie Peterson, Youth Pastor, Brownsville Assembly of God
(Pensacola, FL)

"The most misunderstood and underestimated thing in all mankind is
LOVE. Jenny has been anointed to break down the walls of divorce
piece by piece, bringing the reader back to an understanding of the
Love that God has for us and how we can then love others. This book
is a step by step guide to hope for those hurt by the grips of divorce." -
Matt Swaggart, creator of HoldFast Gear

"ABBA breathes a fresh, encouraging word to the hurting and the
broken. It challenges us to be all that we can be, in spite of the pain,
because of Jesus! Jenny paints a vibrantly passionate picture of a
very present Christ, urging us in the midst of the chaos that divorce
brings, to call out to Him for all the hope that we need. You are
guaranteed to be uplifted, inspired, and bettered from this great read!"
– Dexter Sullivan, Founder, Prayer Power Ministries (Tulsa, OK)

"ABBA takes young people from a posture of being a defenseless
victim of divorce into the posture of being a well-equipped overcomer.
Jenny teaches that we are not merely destined to adjust to our
situation, but we can allow Jesus to take the broken pieces of what
is left and create something brand new and even better than before."
-Jamie Jones, Minister, Jamie Jones Ministries (Tulsa, OK)

"Everything about ABBA is powerful. Divorce is a subject that hurts too
many people but is talked about very little. The Word of God says that
we overcome by the word of our testimony and that is exactly what
this book is. ABBA will shake the world." – Max Kutz, Worship Leader/
Creative Director

"Jenny Kutz's book, "ABBA", is such an easy and enjoyable read.
It breaks down the Word of God to a level where everyone can
understand it. As a result, people can directly apply it to their lives.
This book is perfect for anyone dealing with the difficulty of divorce.
When reading the book, people will learn that they don't just have
to adjust to divorce, but are made more than conquerors through
Christ Jesus, our Strength, and will overcome it." - Evangelist Freddy
Flanagan, The Cave (Baltimore, MD)

ABBA

by

Jenny Kutz

TABLE OF CONTENTS

FOREWORD

Even if my father and mother abandon me, the Lord will hold me close. Psalm 27:10 NLT

Tragically, there are far too many children who feel abandoned by their parents. The dynamic of "even if" a parent or parents would forsake their children, considered unusual in King David's day, has morphed into the reality of nearly half of all families divided by divorce in ours. We see the toll it has taken everywhere from teen suicides to the fear of commitment. And yet in the midst of this pain God has promised to protect us and teach us what our parents could not.

Teach me how to live, O Lord. Lead me along the right path, for my enemies are waiting for me. Do not let me fall into their hands. For they accuse me of things I've never done; with every breath they threaten me with violence. Psalm 27:11-12 NLT

As the child of parents twice divorced I can assure you, God is more than faithful to love, instruct, lead, and fill every void. I am so thankful that Jenny has taken the time to write a constructive, compassionate guide for the peers of her generation who have known the pain of divorce. This book weaves together scriptures and her personal journey so that you can confidently step onto the right path and into the destiny God has for you.

Yet I am confident I will see the Lord's goodness while I am here in the land of the living. Psalms 27:13 NLT

Lisa Bevere
Messenger International
Best-Selling Author / Minister
Kissed the Girls and Made Them Cry, Fight Like a Girl, Lioness Arising

DEDICATION

To my family, one of God's greatest gifts to me,
and to anyone who has been needing the love of the Father.

ACKNOWLEDGEMENTS

I want to thank my Heavenly Father and my Lord, Jesus Christ. Your faithfulness sustained me and is the reason this book could even be written. You are my Abba. I'll spend my life sharing the love you have so freely given.

To my family, thank you for standing with me in this. Your encouragement has been with me every step. Mother and Steve, your support and love have made me so thankful. Dad and Kindra, thank you for loving me and believing in me. To my siblings: Rachel, Caleb (Baby Kenneth), Lyndsey, Max and Emmie. Y'all are my best friends. I love how we have found God's faithfulness together.

Max, thank you for all your help with this from designing the book cover (Go Max!) and creating the promo video. You are a creative genius. Maybe one day I will be like you! You'll always be my "little" brother and will never forget that dream God gave me where beauty replaced the storm. I see it!

Mimi and Papa, thank you for praying for me. I love y'all so much and am blessed beyond measure to be your granddaughter. You follow Jesus with your lives and have no other desire. Your words of wisdom are found throughout the words of this book. I'm thankful for every moment I get to be around you. They are treasures in my life.

To the rest of my family: I love y'all. Thank you for all your patience and kindness towards me! I see God unfolding beautiful things in your lives and believe you will boldly step into them all with God's great grace. I'm so thankful for my family (Long live fig newtons!).

Tara, I will never forget that conversation on the plane home from Paris that sparked the fire of this message now burning in my heart.

Thank you to my Hart family for becoming my family in Branson and still are. Thank you to Cathi and the Maris family for sharing your testimony. Along with everyone that shared their testimonies!

Thank you Harrison House family for joining together with me in this message! Joyce, Julie, Steve, Christina, Gary. It has been a joy to work with y'all!

Thank you Andrea Graff for editing the beginning drafts of my book. Thank you to Mr. Mason for believing in this from the very beginning and giving me great direction.

To the creative genius, Andrea Howey. Thank you for the illustrations! You have such a gift and I know it will be used to impact so many.

Lisa, thank you for writing the powerful foreword. I love you with my whole heart! You have always encouraged and believed in me.

Thank you to all my friends. My life is overflowing with love from y'all.

And thank you to the reader of this book. My heart is that you know the faithfulness of God more today than you did yesterday.

Love,
Jenny

PROLOGUE

Hi, my name is Jenny. I'm sure what you thought you picked up was a book, but what you're actually holding in your hand is the beginning of a journey. When I imagine someone setting out on a journey, I envision them with their bags packed, ready to embark on an adventure. They have their eyes set on a certain goal, knowing that even though others may have the same end result in mind, no two journeys will ever be the same.

Here we are together, with our bags packed. Page by page, we will take one step closer to our destination, one step closer to our glorious future. I realize my thoughts and ideas won't change anything in your life, but God's will. That's why this book isn't about my ideas or opinions, but rather my firsthand experiences and what I have learned through them from God's Word.

Divorce is an uncomfortable topic that most people don't want to talk about. Yet, it's happening every day, everywhere we look—even in our churches. George Barna recently conducted a study that proves the divorce rate is significantly lower for believing, practicing, born-again Christians than non-Christians. But even though the divorce rate is lower in the church, there's no question it's still present and constantly growing.

The sad reality of divorce leaves those involved dealing with questions like: *Whose fault was it? Could it have been avoided? Did someone just want an easy out? Was there infidelity involved?* The truth is that no matter how these questions are answered, divorce still hurts. Not only does divorce affect the man and woman directly involved, but it also has an impact on their children.

Here are some shocking statistics I found concerning children of divorced parents:

- Half of all American children will see their parents' marriage fail. That means out of every two children, one child's parents are divorced.[1]
- Forty percent of children growing up in America today are being raised without their fathers.[2]
- Children of divorced parents are more likely to end their own marriages later in life, after the example that has been set before them.[3]
- Children of divorced parents are more likely to be unhappy or depressed.[4]
- Children of divorced parents suffer academically. They are less likely to graduate from high school.[5]
- Teenagers of divorced parents are much more likely to engage in drug abuse, alcohol abuse and sexual intercourse than those who have both parents living at home.[6]

After reading these statistics, I have become more aware than ever of the reason God hates divorce. According to these statistics, half of our generation doesn't know what it means to be a father or mother because they didn't have that example set before them.

The way in which they treat their spouse will likely mirror the example set by their parents. That's an intimidating thought!

Satan's plan is to get our generation to fall into his traps, being bound by negative effects of divorce. His primary goal is to steal, kill and destroy. He wants to see more young men become absentee fathers and more young women become distant mothers. He tries to get these young people to believe that their life is over. He tries to convince them that they are excused to act poorly because of what they experienced as a result of their parent's divorce.

Divorce may seem like a hopeless situation, a ceiling limiting a young person's future, but it's not. There is hope, and that hope is in Jesus Christ. I believe with all my heart that children from divorced homes don't have to fall into these statistics. I believe that any void caused by a divorce can be filled by hope in Jesus.

We often hear that the best thing children from divorced parents can do is learn to adjust to their situation. But why should we encourage them to simply adjust when they were destined to overcome? They can overcome any insecurity, anger or pain that they experience after their parent's divorce. How do I know? I've been there, that's how I know. My parents divorced when I was seventeen years old. But now I'm on the other side, proclaiming that God's faithfulness can sustain you and bring you to a greater place than ever before. That's what He did for me!

I don't look at writing this book as an opportunity, but rather a responsibility. It hasn't been an easy book to write, but I knew it *had* to be written. The enemy knows there is a world-shaking destiny in the hearts of young people. God is calling this generation to rise up out of the slums of the enemy and become all that He has destined them to be. Philippians 3:12-14 says it so beautifully for us: "Not that I have already obtained this or am already perfect, but I press on to make it my own, because Christ Jesus has made me his own. Brothers, I do not consider that I have made it my own. But one thing I do: forgetting what is behind and straining forward to what lies ahead, I press on toward the goal for the prize of the upward call of God in Christ Jesus" (ESV).

Together we can press toward the goal that is ahead of us. God has such a wonderful plan for you. This book will take you on a journey in which you will learn about love, forgiveness, healing, and acceptance of new relationships in your life. This is no longer about what happened yesterday; it's about where God wants to take you today. Life is not over. Hope is not gone. The adventure is just beginning!

As God's thoughts begin to change your thoughts, I encourage you to write down anything you feel or think. Allow God to write on the tablet of your heart because His pen is far greater, and His etches are far deeper than any other marking your past has tried to write. Let Him rewrite you.

As a result of your parents' divorce, you may have been hurt and think that life will never be the same. Well you're right! Your life will never be the same. But that doesn't mean it has to be worse than it was before. It can be just as great or even greater. If you allow God, the Great Author, to take over writing your story, the plot will be promising and the conclusion will be exciting (Jeremiah 29:11). Are you ready to let God begin writing your story? Regardless of the details of your parent's divorce or separation, you are now in a place of decision. You can decide to move forward. You can decide to overcome. So let's go!

CHAPTER 1

MY STORY

Growing up, I always imagined my life turning out differently than it did. Isn't that what always happens? We all have a picture of what we think we will be when we grow up: a firefighter, ballerina or an astronaut (that was my dream when I was five). But as time goes on, we realize those things aren't always what we imagined.

It never crossed my mind that one day I would go to two separate homes on holidays. I always thought my parents would be married forever. But like so many others, my parents did not stay married; they divorced when I was seventeen years old. Perhaps your parents were separated or divorced when you were even younger than that.

How old were you when you found out your parents were getting divorced? _____

I vividly remember the day I found out that my parents were getting divorced. Wow, what a day that was! Hearing those words changed my entire world. Maybe you heard words like, "Your

19

mom and I are getting a divorce," or "Your dad and I just can't work it out." Maybe you never heard anything at all. Perhaps one of your parents just walked out one day.

Do you remember the day your entire world changed?_____

What happened?_____

_____

_____

_____

_____

_____

_____

What did it feel like when you found out your parents were getting a divorce? _____

_____

_____

_____

_____

_____

What thoughts were going through your mind when those words were spoken? _____

_____

_____

_____

_____

_____

_____

_____

I can recall every detail of the day I heard the news that my parents were getting a divorce. I thought, *Is this really happening? This isn't supposed to happen to me. This isn't how I thought my life would be. What am I going to do?*

As I sat on the couch, stunned, it seemed like my entire world was crashing around me. I couldn't see the next step to take. I couldn't imagine how I would ever get through that day, let alone the next day or the one after that. It was a painful and strange day. But it was not a hopeless day, because that was the day God truly became my Abba, my Father God.

Abba, Father

God didn't actually *become* my Father that day; He had always been my Father. I just never recognized Him in that role as much as I did that painful August night. During that time, His role as my Heavenly Father became a true reality to me. The same can be true for you.

The word *Abba* is Hebrew for "father." If you were in Israel and heard children calling out to their father, you would hear them cry out, "Abba, Abba! Abba, Abba!" We can utter the same cry to our Father God: "Abba, Abba! Daddy, Daddy!" Whenever we feel hopeless or insignificant, our Heavenly Father wants us to call on His name.

When the word "father" is mentioned, what kinds of thoughts come to your mind? Are they thoughts of anger, hurt and betrayal? Or are they endearing thoughts of protection, safety and strength? (Be honest! This is only between you and God).

_____

_____

_____

_____

_____

It's easy to associate the character of God with that of our earthly fathers. If we were hurt or abused by our earthly fathers, the devil may lie and tell us this is the same way our Heavenly Father treats His children. That is not true! The truth about God is found in scriptures like Psalm 18:30, "God's way is perfect. All the LORD's promises prove true. He is a shield for all who look to him for protection," (NLT) and 1 John 4:8 "God is love" (NLT).

We should never compare God with people; we should always compare God with His perfect Word. If our earthly father is a lot like our Father God, it would only be because our earthly father takes after the characteristics of our Heavenly Father—never the other way around. The Bible says that WE were made in HIS image (Genesis 1:27); it doesn't say that HE was made in OUR image.

God is the perfect Father. He is *your* Father! If you only have one of your parents around after the divorce, God is there to fill the void.

"I am certain that God, who began the good work within you, will continue his work until it is finally finished on the day when Christ Jesus returns" (Philippians 1:6 NLT). God has begun a work in you and He is faithful to complete it. You have been adopted into the family of God (Romans 8:15). You have been adopted! You belong to a family—the family of God - and God *always* takes care of His family.

CHAPTER 2

I'VE BEEN ADOPTED

"For you did not receive the spirit of bondage again to fear, but you received the Spirit of adoption by whom we cry out, 'Abba, Father.'"

Romans 8:15 NJKV

Cathi's Story (in her words)

As a child growing up in Romania, I was abandoned by my family and placed in an orphanage to fend for myself. The events that I experienced throughout my life as an orphan girl living in a nation filled with hatred, led me to trust in a force more powerful than myself, even though I did not yet know "Who" or "What" that powerful force was.

My mother was a high school dropout. In a communist country like Romania, a woman could not expect to make something out of her life without a proper education. As years passed, the dream my mother once had of making a life for herself and her family seemed so distant. The pains of abuse caused by my father led her to insanity.

I still believe she was a good mom; however, with two kids, no home, no husband, and no money, she was unable to keep my brother and me. So the next thing I knew, I was holding onto my crying brother as we watched our mother walk away from the orphanage without looking back.

After a few years of life in a boys and girls orphanage, I quickly realized it was no place for a little girl to live. I was surrounded by people who had given up on life. After two years at that orphanage, I was relocated to an all girls orphanage and separated from my brother, the only family I had left.

As I got older, my father started to take interest in me again. He would come and visit me at the orphanage. After a few visits, I found myself in the back of his horse drawn carriage as he drove me away from the orphanage without telling anybody. It didn't take long for me to realize what was happening. I was being trafficked. Although sex trafficking is very common in third world countries, I never thought my own father would do such a thing.

Thankfully, the hand of my Heavenly Father was upon my life and in every situation He never forsook me. Whether I was being abandoned, sold, or lying in a hospital dying of kidney failure and spinal meningitis, God was with me every step of the way.

God's loving mercy intervened in my life many times, but one time in particular changed my life forever. At the age of eleven, I was told a loving family wanted to adopt me. They were pastors and missionaries to countries all across the world. It was truly a miracle from God!

They tried to adopt me from Romania for over a year. It was a difficult process, but they knew they were supposed to do it. A week before September 11, 2001, they went on a mission trip and planned to come to Romania. After that terrible tragedy took place in the United States on 9/11, all the flights going in and out of Romania ceased. Yet, God worked it out so they could fly back to Romania to get me.

Once they got the paperwork ready to finalize my adoption, the man responsible for signing off on it refused to do so. One night in the midst of this battle, the woman who wanted to be my adoptive mother woke up with a strong sense that she needed to get a certain document signed quickly. This piece of paper had not been asked for up front and it seemed so pointless to everyone, including my lawyers and the governments of both Romania and America. Nobody knew why she wanted this piece of paper signed.

The family traveled all over Romania trying to get that paper signed. Finally, they got it signed. They continued to work on my adoption and eventually made it to the Romanian Embassy. But after all their hard work, the official responded by saying, "We have to turn you down because you don't have a specific document we need."

She asked what that document was. It was the exact piece of paper she had worked so hard to get signed, although neither she nor anyone else knew why she had done so. It was a miracle, but only the first of several to come.

After 9/11, adoptions were completely shut down. The government wasn't even looking at them. But somehow, my file ended up in a pile with all the applications for humanitarian visas, which were only granted in those urgent cases when the child would die soon if he or she didn't get adopted. Still, even those with extreme cases weren't being signed off on automatically at that time.

God is so good! One morning, a couple of weeks after September 11, 2001, the papers for my visa miraculously got signed. By this time, the missionary family had already gone back to America because nothing was happening. They were ecstatic when they received a piece of paper in the mail—my signed humanitarian visa! Nobody knew how it got there or how it got signed.

They came back to Romania to get me and once we made it from Romania to the Houston airport, an official asked, "Can we talk to you for a minute?" The officials were confused and asked, "How did you get this girl out?" This was the fourth attempt the missionary family had made to get me to the United States from Romania.

My new family just said, "We don't know, you have the paperwork. You tell us."

The official replied, "This is impossible—all this paperwork, the way it was done, everything. It should have been impossible to get this girl out! I don't know how you did it, but just go ahead. Take her and pass through." Nobody knew how it all happened, but of course God knew. He had His hand on my life the entire time!

As I continued going to church with my new family, I really began to pay attention to the Word of God that was brought forth. It didn't take long for me to realize that throughout all the circumstances in my life, the "Higher Power" that protected me and loved me was the Almighty Creator of the universe.

I received Jesus Christ as my Savior at the age of eleven and have never been the same since. Yes, I have made mistakes in my lifetime and have fallen short, but I know without a shadow of a doubt that my Savior will never leave me nor forsake me.

Wow! Whenever I read Cathi's story, I am reminded of how special she is. Why? *She was chosen!* Out of so many children who could have been adopted, she was the one picked to be loved, cared for and protected. When I heard this same story from Cathi's adoptive father's point of view, I recognized a love in him that's similar to our Heavenly Father's love for His children. Cathi's adoptive father desired for her to get out of that terrible place she was living in and take her home to a better place. He did everything in his power to save her from a life of sadness. He traveled to the other end of the earth just for her. He snatched Cathi out of darkness and placed her in a life filled with hope.

Just as Cathi was rescued from the darkness, God has snatched all of His children out of darkness, sadness and fear, and placed us in safety. That's what it means when the Bible says we have been adopted. We have been rescued. We are now safe. God sent His only begotten Son, Jesus, to rescue us so He would be able to call us His children. "For he has rescued us from the kingdom of darkness and transferred us into the Kingdom of his dear Son" (Colossians 1:13 NLT). No other love is more amazing than the love of our Father God.

My Father Loves Me

I remember once being face-to-face with a woman who was thinking about ending her life. She came up front in response to an altar call given in the service and told me that suicidal thoughts continually plagued her. She felt like she didn't measure up to

30

anyone's standards. She kept saying, "I don't deserve to be taken care of because of all the things I have done. I've let my husband down. He works so hard to care for me, but I have only let him and my children down." She went on and on about her past mistakes and failures.

I began to minister to her and share God's forgiveness and grace. Even though I explained God's wonderful promises to her, she kept repeating her mistakes, failures and unworthiness. Even though God's freeing truths were being shared, her own thoughts kept her from receiving them. I felt like I was getting nowhere. No matter what I said, she kept telling me all the reasons why she was "unworthy."

Finally, in the middle of one of her rants about her mistakes and failures, the Spirit of God rose up in me and I asked her directly, "Did you know that your Father God loves you?"

Suddenly, silence took the place of our conversation. I could tell this question hit her like a ton of bricks as a sense of calmness rushed over her and she realized she had a Father who loved her so much. After a while, she managed to whisper, "My Father loves me."

I said, "Yes, just let that sink in. Let's say it again."

Every time she repeated this, healing and love began to stir in her heart. The more she let the truth sink in, the more she believed it. All the previous talk of what she had done stopped, and now only the goodness and forgiveness of God were on her lips. I gave her scriptures on God's love and continued to encourage her.

She wasn't truly able to receive God's forgiveness and grace until she realized the truth of His love for her. *My Father loves me.* Those four words changed the entire course of her life. God's love plunged to the depth of her human heart to rescue her. I believe she's alive today because of the power of God and the revelation of how precious she is to Him. She changed when she began to see God, not as an impersonal being, but as a Father who knows her every mistake and still loves her dearly. She began to see God as a Father she could run to and trust.

You were also chosen by God to be the one whom He loves and protects. Just look at what Jesus said in John 15:16, "You didn't choose me. I chose you" (NLT). He chose to love you just the way you are. You may feel like you don't deserve to be loved, accepted or taken care of because of things in your past, but your past doesn't change the way God feels about you or His commitment to take care of you. In fact, He already knew you were going to make the mistakes you made and He still chose to love you.

God's love is deeper than any other love you will ever find. No matter how high or how low you go, *nothing* can separate you from His love. You can't run away from His love, even if you tried. He will *always* love you, whether you choose to love Him back or not. But even though His love is so great, He still gives you the choice to accept it. He lets you decide if you will call Him "Father."

If you are ready to see and experience God as your loving, ever-good Father, read Romans 8:15 again, but this time fill in the blanks with your name. Read it aloud this way again and again and again. "For _____ has not received the spirit of bondage again to fear, but _____ has received the Spirit of adoption whereby _____ cries, Abba, Father...Daddy, Daddy" (emphasis and paraphrase mine).

Do you see how precious you are to God? You are so precious to Him that He made a way for you to call Him "Father." This is truly awesome. I remember crying out to God when I was hurting one night, and He showed me a picture of myself as a little girl. I saw myself running into His arms. It wasn't a leisurely jog; I was running full-speed, wholeheartedly into His arms. I never turned around. I just kept my eyes completely focused on Him.

When I finally reached Him, I could sense Him smiling at me. I could feel the love in Him. He picked me up and swung me around and around, just like a daddy would do with his little girl. When the spinning stopped, He placed me on His lap. I remember feeling so innocent, so secure. All of my fears and worries melted away in His great love. That's the kind of father God longs to be to us.

As I grow older, I am determined to keep a childlike faith that will take every opportunity to both cry out to and run to my Heavenly Daddy. Close your eyes and picture God taking you up in His loving arms. Let all fear and shame melt away in His presence. Give Him all your worries and let them fade away.

What does it feel like when you are in God's arms? Do you feel secure? Do you feel safe?

_____

_____

_____

Whenever fear starts to set in or worry starts to overtake you, let His love overwhelm you. Take a look in your heart. What feelings or thoughts are bothering you?

_____

_____

_____

Let Father God be Abba, Daddy to you. Anytime you begin to worry about a situation in your life, just say out loud, "My Father loves me. My Father loves me." Let those words resonate in you.

The Acceptant Father

You may feel like you have messed up so badly that God could never love you again. You may think you have said too much, done too much, or perhaps not done enough to receive His love and acceptance. If that's you, realize that you're not the only one who has ever thought that. You know who else did? The Prodigal Son in the Bible thought that too (Luke 15:11-32).

In this story, we see a young man who begged his father to give him his inheritance money. Once he got it, he packed up and left town, ready to party. He wasted all of his money on living wildly and doing things that would not have pleased his father. He got so low that when he was forced to begin taking care of pigs to make money, he was thrilled at the thought of eating out of their feeding trough. Now that's low—getting excited for some pig slop! But in his destitute state, nobody gave him anything.

One day, he thought back to his father and his home and decided to go back. But this time, he didn't expect to be welcomed as a son; he was just hoping to be accepted as a servant. "When he came to himself, he said, 'How many of my father's hired servants have bread enough to spare, and I perish with hunger! I will arise and go to my father, and will say to him, "Father, I have sinned against heaven and before you, and I am no longer worthy to be called your son. Make me like one of your hired servants"'" (Luke 15:17-19 NKJV).

As the prodigal son journeyed home, imagine the thoughts he had. He was probably thinking about what it would be like when he saw his dad. He may have been thinking about what his dad would say to him. I'm guessing the thoughts he had weren't pretty. But to his surprise, the reaction of his father was the complete opposite of what he expected.

The Bible says that even while the son was still far off, His dad ran to meet him and kissed him. His father had such great love and compassion toward him that he couldn't wait until he reached the house. After his son gave his spiel, the father said to his servants: "Bring out the best robe and put it on him, and put a ring on his hand and sandals on his feet. And bring the fatted calf here and kill it, and let us eat and be merry; for this my son was dead and is alive again; he was lost and is found" (Luke 15:22-24 NKJV).

What a beautiful picture! The father in that story did not say to the son, "Where have you been? I am going to teach you a lesson for what you did. I am going to keep you in the stable." He did not make his son's life harder because of his actions. Instead, he had a party because his son returned. That is just how our Heavenly Father sees us. The way this father approached his lost son is the same way our Father approaches us. He was just glad His lost son had been found.

Have you ever done anything that made you think you were no longer worthy to be called God's son or daughter? Have you ever thought you were unworthy of His acceptance? No matter what you have done, your Father will always open His arms wide to you. When He sees you coming back, He will always run to you. God is not angry with you. He will rejoice over you because you have returned. Psalm 68:19 says that each day, He carries you in His arms. So crawl back up into His lap. Let Him carry you. Let His joy take the place of your sadness.

When your Father God adopted you, not only was room made for you in His heart, but a place was also made in your heart for Him. Does He currently fill that place in your heart? I encourage you to invite Him in. Believe in Him and receive His amazing love.

CHAPTER 3

I Am Loved

"God, your thoughts are precious to me. They are so many! If I could count them, they would be more than all the grains of sand."

Psalm 139:17-18 NCV

God loves you so much that He *always* thinks about you. Do you know how many grains of sand are on the earth? Me neither. In fact, scientists say no one really knows. Recently, the University of Hawaii set out to make an estimate and concluded that there are approximately 7,500,000,000,000,000,000 grains of sand on the beaches of the earth.[7] I didn't even know how to say that number, so I looked it up. Just in case you were also wondering, it is seven quintillion five quadrillion! That, I would say, is a large number. Actually, it's not just large; it's *ginormous*! And that number only takes into account the grains of sand on earth's beaches. Just think of all the sand unaccounted for in the deserts! It's amazing that the thoughts God thinks toward us outnumber all the grains of sand on earth. This means that even if

we live our entire lifetime thinking a new thought every second, we would never think that many thoughts. This realization leaves me in awe every time.

It's astounding that God not only has that kind of time, but that He would want to fill it with thoughts of us. Even before the world was formed, God knew us and loved us. His thoughts have been toward us from before earth's beginning, and they will last far past its existence. He *wants* to think about us and does so continuously.

Maybe you've had thoughts like, *Nobody ever thinks about me. Nobody cares about me, or nobody would miss me if I were gone.* I'm here to tell you that those thoughts are not only destructive, but they are completely untrue. The truth is that God's thoughts are toward you. God cares for you and has a purpose for you to fulfill.

What kind of thoughts do you believe God has about you?

_____

_____

_____

Jeremiah 29:11 says that God has good thoughts about you and your future. He has peaceful thoughts. You are the topic on His mind all of the time.

What do you spend your time thinking about? God? Church? Eating? School? Shopping? Sports? Chocolate (can I hear an Amen, somebody?!)

_____

_____

_____

_____

Whatever you think about is what you are going to talk about. "Out of the abundance of the heart the mouth speaks" (Matthew 12:34 NKJV). So if you are always on the heart of God, then of course He talks about you all the time. The things God speaks about you are kind. His words are life to you. Even though the people you know and love may say hurtful things to you or about you, your Father God never will. He is love, and love is kind.

What kind of words do you believe God says about you?

_____

_____

_____

_____

_____

_____

Here are a few things the Bible tells us God says about you. We know these things are true, because it is impossible for Him to lie. (At the end of this book, these scriptures are written out for you.)

1. You are special. (Psalm 139)

2. I love you forever. (Jeremiah 31:3)

3. My Son Jesus died for you so that I could be your Father You are My child! (Romans 8:15)

4. I have good plans for you and for your tomorrow. (Jeremiah 29:11)

5. Don't worry about anything. Just talk to me, and I'll take care of it. (1 Peter 5:7)

6. I am your friend. I love to talk to you and spend time with you. (John 15:15)

7. I like it when you come to Me. I'll never tell you to go away. (Matthew 19:14)

8. I will never, ever, EVER leave you. (Hebrews 13:5)

9. You are going to make it. In Me, you always win! (1 John 5:5)

10. Does your heart hurt or feel broken? I came to heal you. (Luke 4:18)

Look at all these wonderful things God says about you. He is for you! As I look upon these promises, it makes it easy to rest in His love. It helps me to be still and know that He is God. He is here with me. This causes me to think about Him and realize how much I love Him.

Take a moment to write some things that you love about God. What are some things that you know and love about Him? Warning: You will soon realize there's not enough room on this page, in this book or in a million other books to write out everything that you know and love about God (John 21:25). So if you want, get a notebook and start filling it up!

1. _____

2. _____

3. _____

4. _____

5. _____

6. _____

7. _____

Here are a few that I know and love about God:

1.   He is our Father.

"And I will be your Father, and you will be my sons and daughters, says the LORD Almighty" (2 Corinthians 6:18 NLT).

2.   He is good and only does good.

"You are good and do only good; teach me your decrees" (Psalm 119:68 NLT).

3. **He is a patient Father. He is a kind Father. He never fails us.**

"Love is patient, love is kind...Love never fails" (1 Corinthians 13:4, 8 NIV).

4. **He's not only overflowing with love, but He is Love.**

"Whoever does not love does not know God, because God is love" (1 John 4:8 NIV).

5. **He is El Roi—the God who sees the beginning, the end, and everything in between. He saw us the day we were curled up on the floor with tears running down our faces.**

"The LORD keeps you from all harm and watches over your life. The LORD keeps watch over you as you come and go, both now and forever" (Psalm 121:7-8 NLT).

6. **He hears us. He heard us when we cried out to Him at night.**

"But he most surely *did* listen, he came on the double when he heard my prayer. Blessed be God: he didn't turn a deaf ear, he stayed with me, loyal in his love" (Psalm 66:19, 20 MSG).

7. **He is interested in our lives so much that every moment was written in His book before one of them even came to pass. He knows every thought**

we have and every word we say, even before we say it! He pays attention to us.

"You saw me before I was born. Every day of my life was recorded in your book. Every moment was laid out before a single day had passed" (Psalm 139:16 NLT).

8.   **He is our Protector. He's not here to hurt us, but to save our lives from destruction.**

"Who redeems your life from destruction. Who crowns you with lovingkindness and tender mercies" (Psalm 103:4 NKJV).

9.   **He is our Restorer.**

"He restores my soul...Create in me a clean heart, O God, and renew a steadfast spirit within me" (Psalm 23:3, Psalm 51:10 NKJV).

10. **He is faithful. Whatever we put in His care, He is faithful to perfect and complete.**

"The LORD will perfect that which concerns me; Your mercy, O LORD, endures forever; Do not forsake the works of Your hands" (Psalm 138:8 NKJV).

When you understand how good God truly is, it becomes easy to trust Him with your life. You can be confident in giving your heart to Him when you know how much He loves you and cares for you. He is the Love that protects, the Love that defends, the Love that fights for you, and the Love that makes everything all right.

No matter what you have done or what situation you are currently facing, your Father God has a love for you that does not depend on anything you can do. His love has no terms. "But let all who take refuge in you rejoice; let them sing joyful praises forever. Spread your protection over them, that all who love your name may be filled with joy" (Psalm 5:11 NLT).

Do you believe these things about God to be true? Do you believe He loves you? _____

Pray this prayer with me:

Dear Heavenly Father, I thank You for Your promises to me. I thank You that You gave your Son, Jesus, so You could call me Your child. I am adopted! I am Yours. You reached to the lowest depths just so You could rescue me from the struggle I was in, and You transferred me to a place of promise. Father, thank You for redeeming my life from destruction. My life is not over. You have good plans for me. You have plans of hope for me. You have plans to give me a good future. No matter what has happened in the past, Your love is what carries me through today and what brings me to tomorrow. With my whole heart I trust You, Lord. I know You are faithful to complete the work You have started in me. I am always aware of Your promises to me. I am confident that Your Word will come to pass in my life. I thank You for all of this. In Jesus' name, Amen.

CHAPTER 4

EMOTIONS

Emotions come from God, but so often we misuse them and allow them to get in the way of what He wants for our lives. Sometimes our emotions block the intentions God has for us. When your parents decided to get separated or divorced, a flood of emotions probably rushed in. Those feelings of sadness, hurt and anger are normal. In fact, they are almost unavoidable because you are human. Initially it is not wrong to feel those things, but you cannot let them take over and control you. You must realize that God has given you the power to rule your emotions.

Getting Dressed for Battle

The devil likes to keep "strongholds" in our lives. One of the greatest weapons he has is to get a *strong hold* on us. This is not God's desire for our lives. He has destined us to be overcomers. "For the weapons of our warfare are not carnal but mighty in God for pulling down strongholds" (2 Corinthians 10:4 NKJV). We can only pull off these strongholds of emotion by using the weapons that have been given to us by our Heavenly Father. He has given us all of His mighty, invincible armor. We already have what we need to win! We will never lose when we use these weapons. It's our responsibility to use all of these weapons and fight with them.

This reminds me of the story of a man standing in the freezing cold, holding a warm coat. He says, "It's so cold! I just can't get warm," while all the time he is holding what could be the answer to his problem. He just needs to put the coat on.

Likewise we may say, "I am losing this battle. I just can't win," even though we have the armor of God that guarantees our victory. We simply have to make the choice to put that armor on. Not only must we use these weapons that God has given us, but we must also be fierce in using them. We are mighty warriors. I believe the time has come for us to rise up and take our place. No longer can the enemy keep us back from the purpose that we have been called to fulfill. We will no longer believe the lies of the enemy.

We must always believe the Word of God. That is our sword. We trust in His righteousness because He has made us righteous. That is our breastplate. We have confidence in His peace. That's our warring shoes. We believe what He says to us is true. That is our belt. We have faith in Him. That's our shield to keep us safe from the enemy's fiery darts. God has given us salvation. That is our helmet. When we have done all to stand, we must keep standing. We are warriors of the Most High God. He's on our side, and if God is for us, who can be against us?

Tackling Your Emotions

When I think of the word "tackle," I automatically think about football. Neither my high school nor college had football, so I have always been a little behind when it comes to understanding the game. Yet, I'm still smart enough to know that when another player gets tackled, he gets taken down.

I don't think any huge football player would just skip across the field singing, "Mary Had A Little Lamb" while gently pushing the opposing player down. As hilarious as that would be, it would not cause the other player to fall, unless he fell to the ground laughing (which is probably what I would do if I saw a huge football player skipping across the field singing a lullaby). It just doesn't work that way. In order for him to tackle the other player, he has to be aggressive. He has to put all of his force and effort into the tackle. He must be more aggressive than the player on the opposing team if he wants to take him down.

This is the same approach we must take to overcome our emotions. We must be aggressive in taking our emotions down. They are *not* on our team. We must go in for the tackle and be forceful! We must be prepared to go at it with our whole heart. If we don't go in with that aggressive approach, we will be no more effective than the frolicking football player and our emotions will tackle us. Which player are you?

I'm Sad

Sadness is a common emotion. As understandable as this emotion may be, it is one that holds so many back. If it is not tackled, it may be the vehicle that takes us off course for the rest of our lives. This is not the plan God desires for us. He says He will turn our mourning into joy (Jeremiah 31:13). His Word says that we can rejoice in Him always (Psalm 32:11). It's possible to overcome sadness. It might not be easy, but it is possible and well worth the effort.

When I think about someone who overcame sadness, I think of the story of Ruth. Naomi had two daughters-in-law: Orpah and Ruth. They were married to Naomi's sons for about ten years before both the sons died. In that day if a woman became a widow at a young age, she was supposed to marry the next son in line, her deceased husband's brother. Naomi, however, had no other sons for these ladies to marry, so she released her daughters-in-law to return to their fathers' homes. She probably said something like, "Go on and live your life. I'm an old widow. You won't want to wait for me to have another son. Go and make a new life for yourself."

The reaction the two daughters-in-law had to their release was very different. Orpah took the ticket out and went back to her people. Ruth, on the other hand, decided to dedicate her life to Naomi and to Naomi's God. Ruth sowed in tears, yet reaped in joy (Psalm 126:5). She said, "Entreat me not to leave you, Or to turn back from following after you; For wherever you go, I will go; And wherever you lodge, I will lodge; Your people shall be my people, And your God, my God" (Ruth 1:16 NKJV).

Ruth was determined not to dwell on her sadness, but to be faithful in the midst of it. Even though Naomi was overtaken with sadness, we never see Ruth in this position. Surely she was aware of God's love, because she made the decision to stay with Him. She went wherever Naomi went and praised the God Naomi praised. She diligently served her mother-in-law. Ruth trusted God to provide and was willing to serve Him.

Ruth was joyful and full of hope, despite her circumstances. Her joy was found in God and in serving Naomi. That joy was the power that sustained her. A life full of sadness is a life emptied of strength, but a life full of joy is a life full of God's strength. The Bible says in Ecclesiastes 3 that there is a time for sadness. This means that crying and being sad is not wrong, but staying that way is.

Sadness is a weapon the enemy uses to stop us from using our strengths and fulfilling our purpose. When Jesus died on the cross, Isaiah 53:4 says that He carried our grief and our sorrows. He carried them for us so we would no longer have to. It's too big of a burden for us to bear, so we must have faith in what Jesus did for us on the cross. Then, even when sadness is present, our faith in Him will overcome it. "Don't be dejected and sad, for the joy of the LORD is your strength!" (Nehemiah 8:10 NLT).

The reality may be that life as you knew it, has completely changed. Most likely you will never have a holiday again in which your entire family will be together. Separate Christmases, visits, and family events are all reminders of your parents' divorce or separation. This is a sad thought, but it doesn't have to be on your mind all the time. You have the ability to choose what thoughts you will dwell on. You have the will to decide what to think.

To tackle the emotion of sadness, you must renew your mind and thoughts with the Word of God. "[You] Fix your thoughts on what is true, and honorable, and right, and pure, and lovely, and admirable. [You] Think about things that are excellent and worthy of praise" (Philippians 4:8 NLT, emphasis added). Later this same chapter says, "Rejoice in the Lord always, and again I say, Rejoice" (Philippians 4:4 KJV).

You can always choose to find joy, even in the midst of your circumstances. You can find that joy in the presence of God. In Psalm 43:3-5, the psalmist encourages himself in the Lord. He asks himself, "Why should I be sad? Why am I so discouraged? I know God! I know joy!" When we get into God's presence, we are with the Source of all joy.

Whenever you feel sad, run to God. Whenever you feel discouraged, go to His Word and find out what it has to say about your situation. In God's presence, you will be refreshed. In His presence, you will be strengthened. So don't be discouraged. God-given joy is a joy that no one can take away from you. It's a joy that no situation can take away from you. No matter what happened in the past or what is happening now remember, you have a joy that no man can steal - the joy of your salvation. To remind yourself of this joy, pray this prayer with me:

Dear Heavenly Father, I believe in You and in Your Word. I know that You have saved me. I am joyful because of Your salvation. Lord, help me to use joy as a weapon to overcome the darkness and depression surrounding me. Your Word says that in Your presence is fullness of joy (Psalm 16:11). Thank You for Your presence in my life. I know that whenever I start to get discouraged or dismayed, Your presence will bring me strength and joy. I will never run away from it, Lord. I am an overcomer! Thank You for being with me. Because You are here, I have joy. In Jesus' name, amen.

It's My Fault

Many of us grow up thinking that our parents' separation or divorce was our fault, but that is never the case. They made that decision on their own. It wasn't made because we were not good enough, smart enough or beautiful enough. It was a decision that they made for their own reasons. We must realize that this is the truth and keep ourselves free from any thought that tries to convince us otherwise. "So Christ has truly set us free. Now make sure that you stay free, and don't get tied up again in slavery to the law" (Galatians 5:1 NLT). We must cast down every thought that presents itself that is contrary to what we know to be true (2 Corinthians 10:5).

I Can't Move On

Have you ever felt like you just couldn't move on? Have you ever said aloud that you didn't think you could move on? You must realize that this is a complete lie from the enemy. He wants to keep you in your past, but staying in the past is like staying in chains. You're not free. You're incapable of moving anywhere. That's not a victorious life, but sadly, it's a life so many choose to remain stuck in.

One of my dear friends, Terri Savelle Foy, wrote a book called *Make Your Dreams Bigger Than Your Memories.* In this book, Terri addresses the issue of breaking free from your past. One thing she points out is that you can only conquer your past by focusing on your future. How true this is! We should all live the motto that Paul lived and focus all we are on this: "Forgetting the past and looking forward to what lies ahead, I press on" (Philippians 3:13-14 NLT).

The greatest memory we have of how life used to be cannot even compare to the future God has in store for us. "Eye has not seen, nor ear heard, nor have entered into the heart of man the things which God has prepared for those who love Him" (1 Corinthians 2:9 NKJV). This alone is encouraging, but it gets even better. Many people stop reading here, thinking that they can never discover the magnitude of His plan until they get to heaven. But if you keep reading, it explains that He reveals this glorious plan to us through His Spirit. He *wants* to reveal it to us now!

So now, with your eyes set forward, look to the wonderful things ahead of you. You cannot change your past. You personally cannot undo what has already been done; it is not in your power to do so. But you can determine how you take on your future. It's time to change your thoughts and let them line up with the Word of God. It's time to begin to dream again.

Just Hold On

In Genesis 37, Joseph had a dream that one day his brothers would bow down and serve him. When he shared this dream with his brothers, they became jealous and attempted to kill him by throwing him into a deep well. Instead of going through with the murder however, Judah, Joseph's brother, suggested they sell him to Ishmaelite traders. The brothers agreed and sold Joseph for twenty pieces of silver.

What do you think Joseph was thinking as he was sold? He had just had the dream that his brothers would serve him, but instead they were selling him! I'm sure he had his doubts about God's plan prevailing. Still, he chose to do what we're all called to do in the midst of a battle— *hold on!*

When Joseph arrived in Egypt, the Ishmaelite traders sold him to Potiphar, the captain of Pharaoh's guard. While Joseph was there, he found favor with Potiphar. "The Lord was with Joseph, so he succeeded in everything he did as he served in the home of his Egyptian master" (Genesis 39:2 NLT). Potiphar kept promoting Joseph until he was put in charge of Potiphar's entire household and everything he owned. The realization of Joseph's dream started to look a little closer than it did in that well. He was finally getting somewhere, but shortly after his promotion, Potiphar's wife wrongly accused him and he was sent to prison. So there he was, in the slums of prison. I'm sure the dream was still resonating in his heart, but he may have been wondering if it was really from God.

Joseph continued to be faithful where he was. As he did, God continued to be faithful to him. Even in prison, Joseph was constantly promoted until he was put in charge of the other prisoners. While in prison, he met the king's cupbearer and baker who were imprisoned for offending Pharaoh. They both had dreams that Joseph was able to interpret accurately after he prayed for wisdom. The cupbearer's life was saved and the baker's lost, just as he had interpreted. When the cupbearer was released from prison, Joseph thought that would be his ticket out so he asked the cupbearer to mention him to Pharaoh.

The cupbearer didn't fulfill the request as soon as Joseph would have liked. It wasn't until two years later that the cupbearer finally remembered him when Pharaoh had a dream that no one could interpret. During those two years, Joseph remained faithful, with the dream of his brothers still lingering in his heart.

Finally, Pharaoh summoned Joseph, who again, accurately interpreted a dream using God's wisdom. Pharaoh's dream foretold a seven-year famine that would follow a seven-year surplus in the land of Egypt. Pharaoh ended up putting Joseph in charge of the entire nation. He became second, only to Pharaoh!

When the seven-year famine came, Egypt was the only place where people in the surrounding areas could go to buy food. It was then that Joseph's brothers were sent to Egypt to purchase food for their families. Joseph finally saw his dream come to pass. His brothers bowed down before him with their faces to the ground. The dream that had looked impossible actually came to pass!

All the circumstances Joseph went through could not keep him from the dream God had destined for him. God's hand was on his life, maneuvering him to the place of his fulfilled dream. Still, Joseph had a part to play. What if he hadn't remained faithful where he was? What if he hadn't listened to the Lord regarding the dreams he interpreted? The story would have been very different if Joseph had not held onto the dream God had given Him. What dream has God placed in your heart? Hold on tight and don't let go. For He, the Lord, will bring it to pass in due time (Isaiah 60:22).

Have you let any dreams slip away after your parents separated or divorced? If so, what are they?

_____

_____

_____

_____

We are meant to shine. We are meant to make a difference. The Bible says that we are to go from faith to faith, from glory to glory. With each step, God wants to take us higher. He wants us to progress, not digress. Make the decision today to let the past stay in the past, and to look to God for your future. Let those dreams come alive, like a fire that cannot be quenched Anytime you start to grow discouraged about your future, take a moment and pray this prayer:

Dear Heavenly Father, Your Word says that You know the plans for my life (Jeremiah 29:11). They are good plans. They are plans of hope. I believe that with all my heart. Lord, help me to dream again. Open up the eyes of my heart to see the wonderful things You have for me (Ephesians 1:19). I am ready to move into the things You've prepared for me. I am looking to what's ahead, forgetting my past and moving forward. Anything that's happened to me, anything that I've done, I completely forget. I take on Your thoughts about me. I take on Your thoughts for me. I trust You with my life. In Jesus' name, amen.

I'm Angry

Anger is a cry heard far too often. We say, "Oh, it's okay to be angry. Someone did me wrong. It's only right for me to be angry with them." Well, that's partially correct. It's okay to get angry. In fact, according to the Bible, initial anger isn't wrong if we're angry for the right reasons. It becomes wrong when we allow that anger to cause us to sin, or when we choose to stay angry. This is where we miss it. "'Be angry, and do not sin': do not let the sun go down on your wrath, nor give place to the devil" (Ephesians 4:26-27 NKJV).

In Mark 11, Jesus saw people using the temple for things other than God's purposes and it made Him angry. He overturned the tables of the moneychangers and drove out those who were buying and selling. Then He went on to describe the purpose behind His actions, saying to them, "Is it not written, 'My house shall be called a house of prayer for all nations'? But you have made it a 'den of thieves'" (Mark 11:17 NKJV).

Jesus was angry because the temple of God was being used for unholy things. His love for God and His people consumed Him. But Jesus didn't remain angry with these people. He went on. He let go of his anger. He gave it to God.

When we remain angry, we give the devil a place to interfere in our lives. We give him a "foothold." A foothold is a place or support for the feet, a place where a person may stand or walk securely, or a firm basis for further progress or development. When we remain angry, we give the enemy access into our lives.

Look at the lives of Cain and Abel as recounted in Genesis 4. Abel gave an offering that pleased God, while his brother Cain gave an offering that was unacceptable. Cain became angry with Abel, so God said to him, "You will be accepted if you do what is right. But if you refuse to do what is right, then watch out! Sin is crouching at the door, eager to control you. But you must subdue it and be its master" (Genesis 4:7 NLT). Instead of changing his ways, Cain remained angry and murdered his brother. Sin controlled him.

Even if at first your anger is justified because of wrongdoing, if you remain angry with someone, you will become the one in the wrong. It is time for you to release the hatred you have toward your mom, dad or anyone else who has done you wrong. Resentment only hurts *you*. Make a decision to release your anger today. As unpopular and unaccepted as this view is, it is the truth. Until you accept it and obey it, you can never be free. The only hope you have to attain freedom is to love and forgive.

CHAPTER 5

FORGIVENESS

So far, we've come a long way on our journey. But in order to continue, there's one thing we can't go on without—a forgiving heart. Oftentimes, this is where we end our journey, simply because we are not willing to forgive. The truth is that no matter what the situation is or who the person is who may have wronged us, unforgiveness doesn't affect anyone else but us. Just like the other emotions mentioned, unforgiveness can keep us from the things God has designed for us. The only way to stop the cycle of anger is to make the bold decision to forgive. Forgiveness frees us from *all* anger, *all* bitterness and *all* hatred. It brings freedom and victory.

What Does It Mean to Forgive?

We all have different definitions of the word "forgiveness." We may say we have forgiven, but by what definition?

What is your definition of forgiveness?

_____

_____

_____

_____

Webster (you know, the guy who wrote the dictionary) says that to forgive someone means that you "cease to feel resentment against" them. In other words, you stop being angry with them for whatever wrong they committed. That seems like a pretty reasonable definition.

God's definition of forgiveness, however, doesn't only include ceasing being angry with someone for the wrong they committed, it also includes actually *forgetting* what they did in the first place. We must wipe it out completely! "I, even I, am he who blots out your transgressions, for my own sake, and remembers your sins no more" (Isaiah 43:25 NIV). God's forgiving heart is proven again in Psalm 103:12 as the author writes, "He (God) has removed our sins as far from us as the east is from the west" (NIV). See how far-reaching God's forgiveness is?

The Bible says God will blot out our sins. To blot something out means to wipe out completely or destroy. Our past has been forgiven. Our sins no longer exist because they have been destroyed by the power of the blood of Jesus Christ. When God sees us, it looks as if we never even sinned.

We see God's unending forgiveness when we look at the life of Jesus. He said, "If you've seen Me, you've seen My Father." When we see the heart of Jesus, we know it is a mirror image of the heart of God the Father. Do you remember when Jesus was being beaten and bruised? The men who crucified Him had such intense anger and resentment toward Him. But His desire was not for them to pay for the sin they committed; His desire was to pay whatever price was necessary for their forgiveness. He paid for their forgiveness, as well as ours, with His precious blood. The whole reason He died was to save *them* and *us!*

Jesus lived out what He preached in the Sermon on the Mount when He said, "You have heard the law that says the punishment must match the injury: 'An eye for an eye, and a tooth for a tooth.' But I say, do not resist an evil person! If someone slaps you on the right cheek, offer the other cheek also" (Matthew 5:38 NLT). When Jesus was being tortured and crucified, He didn't say, "You're going to be sorry when you realize who I am." He didn't even say, "They don't know who they're messing with. I am the Son of God. They are going to pay for what they did to Me." Do you know what He said? He said, "Father, forgive them." When I reflect on the fact that Jesus forgave the very men who killed Him, I am reminded that any situation in my life can be forgiven *and* forgotten.

"Therefore be imitators of God, as beloved children. And walk in love, as Christ loved us and gave himself up for us, a fragrant offering and sacrifice to God" (Ephesians 5:1-2 ESV). We are to imitate our Father by following Christ's example. We are to forgive with a forgiveness that knows no boundaries or conditions.

Yes, May God Forgive Her

One of my favorite stories of forgiveness is found in the life of Corrie ten Boom and her sister, Betsie. Their story is one of love, forgiveness and victory in Jesus Christ. During World War II, the ten Boom family was sent to a concentration camp for helping and housing Jews. They were persecuted, humiliated and terribly abused. You can read about the extraordinary depths of their forgiveness in Corrie ten Boom's book, *The Hiding Place.* In this book, we are told of a time when Corrie ten Boom stood naked with her older sister Betsie, watching a concentration camp matron beat a prisoner.

Corrie cried, "Oh, the poor woman."

"Yes. May God forgive her," Betsie replied.

Even in her greatest time of distress, Betsie was praying for the souls of the brutal Nazi guards. I love that! No matter what situation has occurred in our lives, may we always be able to say as Betsie did, "Yes. May God forgive them." Then we will be able to view the person as though they had never wronged us. That is the way God forgives and that is how we are supposed to forgive our brothers and sisters.

When I think of God's forgiveness, I think about a chalkboard.

Every time we do something wrong, our sin is written on the chalkboard but the notation doesn't stay there for long. Do you know why? It is erased by forgiveness. As soon as we turn our hearts toward God and ask for His forgiveness, any sin that was written on that chalkboard is completely wiped clean by the eraser of forgiveness. It wipes it away, just as if the sin was never even committed. God completely blots out that sin.

God's forgiveness is a powerful force. The marvelous thing about it is that we don't have to simply admire His powerful forgiveness. We have been given the ability and power to forgive in the same way. If forgiveness weren't possible, God never would have commanded us to do it. We can do it with His help. Philippians 2:13 says that God is working in us, giving us the power and the desire to do what pleases Him.

Give the Gift of Forgiveness... To Yourself!

Forgiveness is more of a gift for us than for anyone else. It doesn't seem like it would be that way, since we are forgiving someone else. The truth is that we are the ones who are not free when there is bitterness in our hearts. When we make the choice to forgive, we free ourselves. So don't let yourself dwell in that prison of unforgiveness. It will hold you down and hold you back. Unforgiveness is the seed that grows into bitterness; forgiveness is the seed that grows into freedom. Uproot unforgiveness as quickly as you can so bitterness will not have time to take root and grow in your life.

63

"I am the One who erases all your sins, for my sake; I will not remember your sins" (Isaiah 43:25 NCV). When God erases our sin, He not only forgets it for our sake but for His sake also. As a Father, He doesn't want to think of His children as sinners. He wants to see us as clean. Even though He forgets our sins, sometimes as humans, we like to remember the sins of other people. But if God has wiped our sins clean, who are we to hold someone else's sin against them?

I believe God is calling us all to that place of forgiveness. Let's be real; you were probably hurt when your parents got a divorce. In fact, they may still be saying or doing harmful things to you. But you have the power, with the help of the Holy Spirit within you, to forgive them.

Every story is different. Your mom or dad may be on their seventh marriage. You may think, *I've forgiven them enough already; they have run out of grace in my eyes.* Even if they continue to hurt you, no matter how hard it sounds, you can forgive them. In the Bible, Peter, one of Jesus' followers, asked Him, "Lord, how often shall my brother sin against me, and I forgive him? Up to seven times?" (Matthew 18:21 NKJV).

Jesus didn't say, "Well, seven times is a lot but you can still forgive them. But if they sin against you eight times, they've done too much to hurt you. You don't need to forgive them." Jesus answered them by saying, "I do not say to you, up to seven times, but up to seventy times seven" (Matthew 18:22 NKJV). Basically, it doesn't matter how many times someone sins against you; you are called to forgive them every time.

I remember a time when I thought I had completely forgiven someone who had hurt me. But every time I saw that person or even thought about them, I thought about what they did to me. I realized I had kept a list of their sins toward me. It wasn't on purpose, but I still did it. Every time I saw them, I brought out that list and would think: *They talked about me. They broke their promise to me. They don't really care about me.*

Do you have anyone in your life like that? If so, who is it?

First Corinthians 13 says that love keeps no list of wrongs. We must forgive on purpose and for a purpose. That purpose is to be free. I wasn't free. I remember when God spoke to my heart and said, "Jenny, you haven't really forgiven them."

I thought, *Yes I have. I no longer have resentment toward them for what they did to me.*

God responded, "You haven't forgiven them because when you think of them, you think of what they did. When I forgive, I forget." I finally realized I had not completely forgiven them. Every time I thought of them, I thought of their mistakes. I never separated the sin from their name. It was always connected. In my heart, I knew I had to make the choice to erase that chalkboard of sin. Once I did, I can honestly say that the next time I saw them, the only thing I thought about was how much I loved them. What they did to me never even crossed my mind. Praise God! It *can* be done. But there is only one way, and it is by love.

You may say, "But it's so hard to love them. You don't know what they did to me."

Well, you're right; I don't know what they did to you. I don't know what they said to you. But I do know the One who knows. He is your Daddy God. He's the One who knows every thought you have and knows everything you do. He will help you.

You don't have to love that person with your own human love. Our human love has limits. Our human love makes a list and loves according to that list. When we try to love without the love of God, we are limited. But the love of God has no list and no conditions. "Now hope does not disappoint, because the love of God has been poured out in our hearts by the Holy Spirit who was given to us" (Romans 5:5 NKJV).

God put His own love in our heart. It's true! So if His love is in us, then we, with the help of the Holy Spirit, can forgive and forget. Truly forgiving those who hurt us, no matter who they are, can only happen when we forgive with the matchless love of God. Allow God's love to fill your heart. You no longer have to keep trying to forgive out of your own human love tank. No! You, with the help of the Holy Spirit, are able to forgive and love out of His endless supply. Now, here is *your* chalkboard.

Think of anyone you believe has done you wrong or hurt you. On this chalkboard, write down everything you are still holding on to. Write down any wrong that comes to your mind when you think of that person. Then confess this:

Father God, my Daddy, I come to You in the name of Jesus, believing that what You have said is true. Your Word says that the Holy Spirit has placed Your love in my heart. Lord, I make a decision to love like You love. I make the choice to forgive like You forgive. I choose to forgive _____ . Your love covers their sin. I choose to remember no longer any wrong that has been done by them. Father, I thank You for helping me to continue this journey in complete freedom. I am free in Jesus' name! Amen.

Now as an act of faith, use the love of God that is in your heart to completely erase what you wrote on the chalkboard. There, it's finished! Now you are free in Jesus' Name! You're free from bitterness. You're free from anger. You're free to live without anything holding you back. You're above all those emotions and negative thoughts. You have tackled them!

CHAPTER 6

HEALING IN
YOUR HEART

True healing can take place when we take the steps to forgive and forget. Good things can be planted in the soil of our hearts when unforgiveness and bitterness have been uprooted. These good things include the fruit of the Spirit: love, joy, peace, patience, kindness, gentleness, goodness, faithfulness, meekness and self-control (Galatians 5:22, 23).

When our hearts are clear of bitterness, the Word of God is able to take root and produce the fruit of the Spirit in our lives. It makes all the difference when our hearts are rooted in love instead of hate. Love brings freedom and healing. Now that we have forgiven, our hearts are open for our Daddy God to move. When we cry out to Him with a humble, willing heart, His promise is that He will heal and sustain us, just like He did for David, who said, "O LORD my God, I cried out to You, and You healed me" (Psalm 30:2 NKJV).

It's time for us to move forward on this journey—forgetting the past, forgetting yesterday. It's time to look toward our tomorrow. I know it hurt when you found out your parents were separating or getting a divorce; I've been there. But I want to let you know there's hope. You can no longer focus on how you were hurt; you must now focus on how you can overcome.

There is hope for your heart to be whole again. It may seem impossible at the moment, but nothing is impossible with God. You may say, "I'm too far gone. I've been hurt too much. I've sinned too much. There's just not much left of me for God to work with." Don't forget that He is the God who turned water into wine. He's the One who turned five loaves and two fish into a feast for thousands. He can take a heart that's turned toward Him and do something beautiful with it. Let Psalm 51:10 be your prayer: "Create in me a clean heart, O God. Renew a loyal spirit within me" (NLT). This is your hope!

Ask Jesus into Your Heart

The first step toward your complete healing is to invite the Healer to dwell in your heart. Believe and confess that Jesus Christ is your Lord and Savior. Believe that His promised Holy Spirit will come and make His home in your heart. Do you remember all of those promises mentioned earlier in the book? All of those promises are fulfilled in Jesus. If it wasn't for Jesus, there would be no hope of healing or restoration. Our lives would be a lost cause.

But that's not the case. In Him we find ourselves, and in Him, we can also find our future.

Have you ever asked Jesus to come into your heart to be your Lord and Savior? If you have never done that, take a moment right now to give Him your life. Surrender everything to Him. You *can* trust Him. Pray this prayer out loud:

My Dear Heavenly Father, thank You for sending Your Son, Jesus, to die on the cross for my sins. Thank You for raising Him up so that I can have victory in my life. I believe that. I believe with all my heart that Jesus died on the cross and rose again on the third day. Come into my heart, Lord Jesus. Heal it. Make it clean. I give You everything today. I give You my whole heart. You are my Lord, and I surrender my life to You. Thank You, Father, for calling me Your child. In Jesus' name, amen.*

Guess what? It's that easy. If you prayed this prayer for the first time, this is truly the greatest day of your life! The greatest miracle of all has just taken place. Your life will never be the same. You have a friend who sticks closer than a brother. You have a friend who will never leave you—a friend who is always faithful. That friend is Jesus.

Now that you have invited Him to make your heart His home, He can begin the healing process. Instead of living in a castle, the

---

*If you prayed this prayer for the first time, please turn to the back of the book for details on how to contact us to let us know.

King of all kings decided to make His castle your heart. What an awesome thought!

A Parable: The King Lives Here

Imagine that you just received a call that the King was coming over to visit you at your house. You ask yourself, "Why would He visit my house when He could just stay in His kingdom with servants and maids?" Once the shock settles, you take a survey of the state of your house. Your living room is unorganized. Your kitchen is a mess. In fact, every room has hidden messes with random things stuffed in closets. You may think, *But surely the King won't look there.*

You begin to clean. You hide the dishes from the discount store and put out the fine china. After all, it *is* the King who is coming! He deserves honor and respect. He deserves the best. After hours of scrubbing and cleaning, everything is finally immaculate. Your house is prepared for the King.

Ten minutes before the King arrives, tons of thoughts begin to fill your head. *Why would He come here? What would make Him want to be here?* You know the only way you will find out the answers to these questions is from the King, so you stop thinking and start taking one more look around your house. It looks perfect.

You hear a knock at the door, and your heart jumps. The King is here! You greet Him. He smiles. You invite Him in, still wondering why He would want to come to your house and have dinner with you. As each minute passes, you become a little more curious as to why He came. As the King is enjoying the fine dinner you prepared for him, you smile as you glance over your house.

Then the King asks, "Can I stay here?"

You think, *Did the King really just ask that?* You're a little confused so you ask, "Here? Why would You want to stay here when You could live in a perfect place, a place where You could be served? My place is small. It is not fit for a King."

He responds, "I am here and became King, not to be served but to serve. The place where I live is already perfect. There are no needs there. I asked you to accept My invitation so I could dwell here and make it better. I will bring the finest things of My kingdom into your house. I'll bring My china and My furniture. I will make additions to your house. I will make it fit for a King."

You sit there, stunned. But then you remember the closets and say, "I'm honored that You would not only come to visit, but that You would actually desire to live in my house. But King, I have a confession to make that may cause You to change Your mind. My house is not perfectly clean. There are some corners and closets that are stuffed with junk. I really don't think You would want to live here."

He just smiles and says, "My friend, I am *choosing* to live here. If you let Me, I will come to dwell here. I will clean those hidden storage places out. So I will ask you again, Can I stay here?"

Finally, you respond, "It is my joy and honor to say, 'Yes of course!'" Then the biggest smile comes across your face as you realize the *King* lives here!

The Moral

Isn't this what Jesus, the King of kings, does for us? We are His temple, His dwelling place. He didn't come just to visit, but to stay. How often do we hide things? How often do we act as though He is just coming for a short visit and won't see the things in our lives that are shameful, things we need to work on? That's what He came to do. We are His holy habitation. He came to fill the most precious parts of who we are with Himself.

Isaiah 6:1 says, "[In a vision] I saw the Lord sitting upon a throne, high and lifted up, and the skirts of His train filled the [most holy part of the] temple" (AMP). He longs to dwell in your home, your heart. He came to fill every part of who you are with everything He is. There is some healing that needs to take place in your heart. That's why He has chosen to live there. He wants to heal you, but you must let Him in!

"The Spirit of the Lord is on me, because I am marked out by him to give good news to the poor; he has sent me to make well those who are broken-hearted; to say that the prisoners will be let go, and the blind will see, and to make the wounded free from their chains" (Luke 4:18 BBE). Jesus said that the Spirit of the Lord was upon Him to heal the brokenhearted, the wounded.

Have you been wounded? Take courage. You are the reason He came.

Making Your Heart His Home

Have you ever created a wonderful drawing on the fireplace with a permanent marker? (Seemed like a good idea when I was two!) Imagine if you spilled soda on your mom's carpet at home. Your mom would probably eventually call someone to come and clean the carpet, but if she had guests who were just about to arrive just after the soda was spilled, she might take the spare rug out of the "junk" closet and cover up the stain.

When your mom's special guests arrived, even though the stain was covered up, you know she would still be mindful of what was hidden underneath that rug. She would probably be thinking, *What if they see the stain under this rug? Will they think less of me?* But still, she would put on a smile, hoping they wouldn't notice or ask.

To her surprise, perhaps every guest complimented her on the beautiful rug in the middle of the room. Perhaps they exclaimed, "What a beautiful place to put a rug. What a stunning decoration!" Every time someone made a comment, she would be reminded of the stain. The stain was still there; she was just hiding it, covering it up so no one would notice. Instead of enjoying her party, she would only have the stain on her mind.

Did you know that we can do the very same thing with our hearts? When I began writing this book, this happened to me. Writing this book required me to dig into a tender place of my heart, a place that was broken. It was a place in my heart that I had covered up with a "rug." But guess what? That rug didn't remove anything. The stains were still there; they just weren't visible to anyone except God and me. I knew they were there and so did He.

One "rug" in our lives might be turning a blind eye to a situation when God tries to heal the stain. When I was in college, I struggled with an eating disorder. I never went to the doctor to get a diagnosis, but I knew in my heart there was a place in my life that I wasn't letting God take control of. When you have an eating disorder, you are taking control of your own body in your own way. God always does a better job handling our lives than we do. That's why it is so important to surrender our entire lives, every detail, to Him.

When I first began to deal with this eating disorder, I started by running. I really enjoyed running and found myself on the track every day. Of course, running is a great way to work out and get healthy, but I was not eating enough calories for the amount of energy I was exerting. During this time, I never ate three complete meals a day and when I did eat, I only ate very minimal amounts. I also supplemented one of my daily meals with an energy bar. My eating habits, along with my exercise routine of running six to ten miles every day, were very destructive to my body.

I struggled with my weight my entire life and thought I had finally found something that worked. I began to lose weight so I was happy. When I was growing up, I always had extremely thick hair. My mom used hairspray and a comb to make my hair "bigger than Texas" (and that is BIG!). But now because of my unhealthy habits, I was losing my hair in chunks. My thick hair became thin. I couldn't even pull it back without my scalp showing. For a college-age girl, that can be frightening.

During that time I reached the size I always wanted to be, but now that I was there, I was paranoid about not gaining any weight so as to remain that size. I kept eating and exercising the same way I had been, never letting God heal places that could only be healed by His power.

One night, God woke me up at 3 a.m. and sternly said, "You need to do something about this." That was my wake up call. Later that day, I called my mom and confessed what I had been struggling with. She prayed with me and bound the spirit of fear that was working in me. That day, I let God in to do some major reconstruction and restoration in my life.

It truly was a miracle that I came out of that tough time in such a victorious way. During my restoration process, I remember asking my family at dinner, "Is this a normal amount to eat? I don't remember." Being restored can be a humbling thing, but it is worth the journey. Pride keeps people living in sin with a hardened heart. I like what Keith Moore says, "Let your hardened heart fall on the Rock of Ages and be broken before God."

True healing requires letting your hard heart be broken before God. The Great Restorer *can* and *will* rebuild you. No matter what the root of my bad decisions might have been - whether it was a struggle to be accepted, feelings of unworthiness, or a desire to be beautiful - I found that God is bigger than any of these things. I just had to let Him remove the "rug" and do His work.

This may be happening to you as you read this book. You may have been digging deep into those places that you have shut off or tried to hide. There may very well be a rug covering up past hurts in your life. What stains in your life have you covered up? What hurts have you not allowed Him to heal? How many times has there been a smile on your face but pain in your heart? What will be revealed when the rugs are removed?

Your heart can never be healed until these things are revealed. Lifting up those rugs isn't always comfortable. Actually, it never is. You're addressing a tender part of your heart, but it's worth it. God has come into your heart to do the work that only He can— healing your broken heart. Now is the time to lift up the "rugs" on the floor of your heart.

When you read that sentence about covering up a hurt, what situation in your life comes to mind? (Don't worry…this is just between you and God.)

_____

_____

_____

Have you covered this hurt with a rug? What kind of rug did you use? A smile? Anger? An eating disorder? Cutting?

_____

_____

_____

_____

I wasn't completely healed until I removed the rug and let Jesus heal me. If you let Him, Jesus will come in and fill every single inch of your heart with who He is. And He is everything you need!

Are you afraid of what will happen to you and your family in the future? Let Jesus fill your heart with *peace*. "For He Himself is our peace…" (Ephesians 2:14 NKJV).

Is your mom or dad not able to pay your bills anymore? He is your *provider*. "He who did not spare his own Son, but gave him up for us all—how will he not also, along with him, graciously give us all things?" (Romans 8:32 NIV).

Are you sad? He fills your heart with *joy*. "The joy of the LORD is your strength" (Nehemiah 8:10 NIV).

Do you feel like you can't make it another day? He fills your heart with *strength*. "Be of good courage, and He shall strengthen your heart, all you who hope in the LORD" (Psalm 31:24 NKJV).

Do you constantly think about how you may never see your dad or mom anymore? Your Heavenly Father is and will always be. "You received the Spirit of adoption by whom we cry out, 'Abba, Father'" (Romans 8:15 NKJV). Don't you see? Jesus is EVERYTHING you need!

I'm More than a Conqueror

You may have come through a storm, but you will come out victoriously. Have you heard of Shadrach, Meshach and Abednego (Daniel 3)? They were three young Hebrew men who were thrown into a fire because they didn't bow down to King Nebuchadnezzar's idol. Jesus came to their rescue in that fire and they were saved. They were victorious!

Those three young men weren't just conquerors, they were more than conquerors (Romans 8:27). Some would say they conquered the fire because they came out alive. I say they *more* than conquered the fire because they not only came out alive, but they came out without even the smell of smoke on them (Daniel 3:27).

You may have recently walked through the fire. With Jesus, you can come out of the fire, not just alive, but unharmed and without even the smell of smoke on you. You are more than a conqueror! Say this out loud: "I am more than a conqueror through Him who loves me. Jesus loves me. I win!"

I Am Restored

"But if we are living in the light, as God is in the light, then we have fellowship with each other, and the blood of Jesus, his Son, cleanses us from all sin" (1 John 1:7 NLT). By the blood of Jesus Christ, we are made clean. His blood has washed us clean. The healing power of His blood has created newness in us. We may have been torn down and battered, but He restored our soul, making us completely new again. He created a clean heart in us. "The LORD is my shepherd; I shall not want. He makes me to lie down in green pastures; He leads me beside the still waters. He restores my soul; He leads me in the paths of righteousness for His name's sake" (Psalm 23:1-3 NKJV).

When I hear the word "restore," I think of a warehouse. If a warehouse is completely empty, it is not fulfilling its purpose. The warehouse manager must replenish and restore the supplies that were lost or sold. That's what our Shepherd, Jesus, does in this healing process. He replenishes those things that were lost. He restores those things that were stolen. He makes us new.

The Bible says that if anyone is in Christ, he is a new creation. Old things have passed away, and all things have become new (2 Corinthians 5:17). Not some things—*all* things! Things in our lives are made new. God gives us beauty in place of our ashes. He gives us joy in place of our mourning. He gives us praise and thankfulness in place of our heaviness (Isaiah 61:3).

In All Things, Be Thankful

"As for me, I will always have hope; I will praise you more and more" (Psalm 71:14 NIV). Thankfulness is another major key to our victory and healing on this journey. Being thankful means being mindful of what God has done. It gets our eyes off of ourselves and onto the goodness of God. Though thankfulness is a vital aspect of our lives, we sometimes forget the power of it. Thankfulness brings us into God's throne room. "Enter into his gates with thanksgiving, and into his courts with praise: be thankful unto him, and bless his name" (Psalm 100:4 KJV).

There is great joy and strength in God's presence. Acts 3:17 says that times of refreshing come from the presence of God. If thankfulness can bring us to that presence, then thankfulness can bring us to joy, strength and healing. "For the Lord shall comfort Zion: he will comfort all her waste places; and he will make her wilderness like Eden, and her desert like the garden of the Lord; joy and gladness shall be found therein, thanksgiving, and the voice of melody" (Isaiah 51:3 KJV).

Take a moment to reflect on your life. Is thankfulness found in it? _____

"All the days of the afflicted [are] evil, and gladness of heart [is] a perpetual banquet" (Proverbs 15:15 YLT). Show me someone who is thankful and I will show you someone who is living victoriously no matter what the circumstances. Let's take a look at the account of the ten lepers who came to Jesus in Luke 17:11-19 (NKJV):

Now it happened as He went to Jerusalem that He passed through the midst of Samaria and Galilee. Then as He entered a certain village, there met Him ten men who were lepers, who stood afar off. And they lifted up their voices and said, "Jesus, Master, have mercy on us!" So when He saw them, He said to them, "Go, show yourselves to the priests." And so it was that as they went, they were cleansed. And one of them, when he saw that he was healed, returned, and with a loud voice glorified God, and fell down on his face at His feet, giving Him thanks. And he was a Samaritan. So Jesus answered and said, "Were there not ten cleansed? But where are the nine? Were there not any found who returned to give glory to God except this foreigner?" And He said to him, "Arise, go your way. Your faith has made you well."

Jesus had done so much for these men. He cleansed their bodies; He healed them. But only one of them returned to give thanks. He was the one who was truly made whole. It is only fitting for us to give God glory for all the good things He has done and has promised to do.

We should not look at other people's lives and say, "Why is my life not like that?" or "Why did this happen to me and not them?" We must look at what God has done for us personally. When we look at good things in other people's lives with envy and jealousy, we shut our eyes off to the good things God is doing in our lives. The person who trusts in himself or other people will not even see when good comes to him (Jeremiah 17). But the man who trusts in God bears fruit even in a drought. It's important to trust God in every circumstance, knowing there is goodness to be found if we just open our eyes and look.

Our faith and trust in God causes us to praise and glorify Him. We worship Him because we know His Word is true. We thank Him because we know He's good. We praise Him because we know He will never fail. If He said it, we believe it. There is no need to fear or worry when we know He's on our side.

If you're ever having a bad day or starting to feel sorry for yourself, just begin thanking God for what He has already done for you. If you can't think of anything to thank Him for, start off by thanking Him for Jesus. Oh my, what can we say about Jesus? He is the most precious thing to us!

You may be facing a huge trial, but be thankful. That's how you come out on top. That's how you come out as an overcomer, completely unharmed by the fire you walk through. Count it all joy because that's where your victory is. Do you want to know how I know that? Second Corinthians 2:14 says, "Now thanks be to God who always leads us in triumph in Christ" (NKJV). God always leads us in triumph! When you are truly thankful for something, you can't contain yourself. If God has done something good for you (which He has), thank Him. Praise Him with your lips. "Has the LORD redeemed you? Then speak out! Tell others he has redeemed you from your enemies" (Psalm 107:2 NLT).

Have you been redeemed? _____

If so, speak out about it. You are coming out of this. You are going to make it. List some things you are believing God for. List things that you have yet to see come to pass in your life and relationships:

1. _____

2. _____

3. _____

4. _____

5. _____

Now, I want you to go back through that list and thank God for each of these things like they have already come to pass. For example say, "Lord, I thank You that You have restored the relationship with my mother." Or say, "Lord, I give You praise for removing all sadness and bitterness from my heart."

Cultivate a life of thanksgiving. Wouldn't it be wonderful if you were known as "the one who is thankful"? That's a great reputation to have! A heart filled with thanksgiving will also cause you to enjoy life and God so much more.

Let praise rise up in your heart so it will come out of your mouth. Out of the abundance of the heart, the mouth speaks (Luke 6:45). Let praise and thankfulness fill up and overflow out of your heart. The things that are coming out of your mouth will reflect victory. If you start to speak victory out of your mouth, you will start to see victory in your life.

I'm Thankful For...

Let's begin to practice this life of thankfulness. Since there is always something to be thankful for, let's think of some of those things. Here are a few examples to help you get started:

1. The fact that you woke up this morning.

2. Jesus.

3. Your little brother. (Hopefully you're thankful for him!)

Now it's your turn. Let thanks flow from your heart. It's never-ending. Once you get started, you'll never be able to stop. "Great is the LORD, and greatly to be praised; and His greatness is unsearchable" (Psalm 145:3 NKJV). Begin this never-ending list with the greatness of God. Whenever you are having a hard day, I encourage you to come back to this list and read it again and again. It will cause you to be mindful of the things God has done and continues to do in your life. Start your list here...

1. _____

2. _____

3. _____

4. _____

5. _____

6. _____

7. _____

8. _____

9. _____

10. _____

11. _____

12. _____

13. _____

14. _____

15. _____

16. _____

17. _____

18. _____

19. _____

20. _____

(There is room in the back of the book if you want to write more.)

CHAPTER 7

HEALING IN YOUR RELATIONSHIPS

G od's power is so great. He is a God of miracles, those that happen instantly as well as those that happen over time. His miracles are all around us, but we must open our eyes to see them. The way we woke up this morning was a miracle. The sun rising was a miracle. When we asked Jesus to come into our lives, that was a miracle, too. The fact that we have been able to forgive the one who has wronged us is definitely a miracle. Healing and restoration of a relationship is one of the greatest miracles of all.

Relationships and friendships may take some time to heal as trust is rebuilt. That's simply because in a relationship, you are dealing with another person. Their will is involved. God has given all of us a free will. As Deuteronomy 30:19 says, we have been given the choice between life and death, between blessing and cursing. Our hearts may be in the right place to bring the relationship back to where it was, but the other person may still have unresolved anger or bitterness. We cannot force them to love us, nor can we force them to want to spend time with us.

What do you do then? Look to the Word of God for your answer. Do what Matthew 5:44 says: "Love your enemies, bless those who curse you, do good to those who hate you, and pray for those who despitefully use you and persecute you" (NKJV). You may say, "I can't do that. It's way too hard." I'm here to tell you that you can. Whatever Jesus has told you to do, He has given you the ability to do, and that ability is found in His grace.

Grace and Peace to You

The grace of God is truly a gift. The only way we can do what He has commanded us to do is through His grace. The word "grace" in the Greek is the word *charis*. It is defined as a gift or blessing brought to man by Jesus Christ; favor; gratitude; thanks; a kindness. You have been given this gift of grace—the gift of being able to accomplish all that you are instructed by God to accomplish, including forgiving one another.

The instruction that Paul wrote to the churches in the letters of the New Testament was not easy to fulfill. Yet Paul still wrote them with full belief that they would fulfill the instruction if they lived their lives through the grace of God. Just look at how he addressed each letter, even before giving any instruction, "To all who are in Rome, beloved of God, called to be saints: Grace to you and peace from God our Father and the Lord Jesus Christ" (Romans 1:7 NKJV). "Grace to you and peace from God our

Father and the Lord Jesus Christ" (1 Corinthians 1:3 NKJV). "Grace to you and peace from God our Father and the Lord Jesus Christ" (2 Corinthians 1:2 NKJV). "Grace to you and peace from God the Father and our Lord Jesus Christ" (Galatians 1:3 NKJV).

This same type of greeting is found in every letter Paul wrote. Not only did he include grace in the beginning of each book, but he also included it at the end of each one as well. He truly recognized the importance of the grace of God. He understood that the assignment God had given him was impossible to fulfill without grace. It is the same way for you and me. Sometimes, forgiveness or restoration of a relationship seems impossible. However, by the grace of God, we can stand and forgive. By the grace of God, restoration can occur in our hearts as well as in our relationships.

The grace of God empowers us. Through grace, we are able to have a relationship with the Father God. It is all because of grace. It's not because of anything we have done or accomplished; it's because of what Jesus did for us on the cross. All we have to do is believe and receive the grace that has been so freely given to us.

What if They Don't Respond?

Every situation is different. Every family is different. Every story is different. That's why it is so important for you to personally hear from the Lord about what to do in your situation. The truth is that not every relationship is restored. You may never have some relationships again. You may never see your father or mother again.

You have to know that even if a relationship is never restored, God *will not* leave you lacking anything. "The LORD is my shepherd; I lack nothing" (Psalm 23:1 NIV).

I believe that if you do what you are supposed to do, which is to love and pray for your enemies, God will honor you. Look at His promise in Psalm 68:6, "God places the lonely in families" (NLT). You may never have a relationship with your earthly mother or father again but you must remember that first and foremost, you have a relationship with your Heavenly Father. This is the most important relationship you can ever have. God promises to place you with a family. I believe He will connect you with someone on earth who can fulfill the needs that aren't being met through your own father or mother.

When I was twenty years old, I moved to Branson, Missouri, by myself. I lived away from all of my family. I had friends in Branson, but it wasn't the same. I remember going home after church one day in tears, because I missed going out to lunch with my family. I began to seek the Lord for comfort, and do you know what He did? He began to bring people to me who treated me like family. I started to spend time at their homes with their family, instead of spending every night alone at my apartment. I became part of a family.

Even now I am a part of that family, even though I do not live near them. God sent me a family when I wasn't close to my own. He placed me in a family when I was lonely. I believe He will do this for you, too. Just believe the promise God has for you. Stand on it. Keep your eyes on Him and He will direct you.

Ashley's* Story (in her words)
(*Name has been changed)

Growing up, my dad wore lots of hats: music minister, family counselor, the man who loved to mow our grass and work outside in the yard, husband to my precious mom, the dad who dressed up (tie and all) to take me out on 'Daddy/Daughter Dates,' lover of all Mexican food and anything with Tabasco sauce on it, world traveler, and the list goes on.

But at 17 years old, I learned about a hat I didn't know my father was wearing and had worn for many years. I found out that my dad was also a functioning alcoholic. The fact that he was "functioning" meant exactly that. He, for the most part, could drink himself drunk but then continue to go to work and live a somewhat normal life. He had developed such a high tolerance for alcohol that he just kept drinking more and more to get to the point of drunkenness. But his alcoholism was beginning to seep through the cracks of his "normal" facade.

Pretty soon after my discovery, Dad started getting arrested periodically. We were constantly hiding his car keys so he wouldn't drive drunk, and he was missing work because of it. He saw no need to change his lifestyle, and my mom just couldn't handle it anymore. In 2005, when I was a junior in college, she sat us down at a family counseling session and told us that she was leaving my dad. I remember everyone crying as we left, my parents in separate cars, appropriately enough. I remember my dad saying, several times, "This isn't what I wanted."

My younger brother and I didn't do much processing together. We basically came to an agreement that family life was increasingly disappointing, and that was that. From that point on, and for several months leading up to it, God opened physical, earthly doors to a home that we could escape to when we just couldn't stand to be in our own home.

Some dear, lifelong friends of ours lived just a few blocks away. They made it clear that we were welcome in their home any time, day or night, and we took them up on it. If we weren't in class or at church, we were there. Their home was always filled with friends who were fast becoming our family. When they moved away a few years later, I wrote this, remembering all the time I'd spent there:

"Imagine a house... no, a home...where anyone is welcome at any time of the day or night—where the scent of freshly baked bread fills the kitchen, and the sound of laughter echoes from the rooms down the hall. Imagine a living room in which the television and the furniture are never the focal point. Imagine a room where people are always welcomed and made

to feel like an invited guest at a 5-star hotel. Imagine that in this living room, people do not gather only to sit and talk (or in many cases, pray) but to circle around the beautiful old piano and harmonize to sing beautiful praise songs to their awesome God. Imagine it as a refuge, a refuge from the changing world around you. Imagine it as a place that, though the paint on the walls changes often, somehow remains the same.

Imagine now that your favorite people in all the world are there at one time or another. Imagine that it was inside those walls that you prayed earnest prayers for fallen believers, dissipating marriages, imprisoned friends, and even addicted family members. It was there that you found warm hugs of comfort and peace during an otherwise inconsistent, tumultuous season of life. This house and the things that took place beneath its roof have helped to shape who you are today.

Imagine sneaking out of your own house after bed to go and be in this refuge. Imagine that it is where you fell in love, and where you first heard the song that one day would be played in your wedding. Imagine that the night you got engaged, this was one of the first places you went. Imagine that in that now empty living room, you used to spend rainy, sticky nights on the couch (or sometimes floor) laughing yourself to sleep.

Imagine being so closely knit to the people in those rooms that you begin to call them your family. Imagine saying you're going home for the night but instead sitting on the front porch in deep conversation for hours after you should have left. Something about this house is magnetic. It draws you in, envelopes you in safety and peace and somehow steals you away for awhile. I know deep down that it is the relationships I share with the people inside that make it that way. I am so thankful for the mark this family has made on my life and on the lives of many people I love so dearly. I'm so thankful that the Lord gave them that wonderful home. They may have seen dozens of things that needed repair, but we only ever saw the love on their faces as we walked through the door."

My parents' divorce was not easy for me. I felt my view of my future had become all but invisible. I questioned the sincerity of every childhood memory, every holiday, vacation and family dinner I'd ever experienced. For a girl who grew up hearing her mom and dad say repeatedly, "Divorce is not an option," all trust had been broken.

None of it made sense anymore, but God was still on our side. God was still moving, working, orchestrating people and circumstances in our lives that wouldn't allow us to run out from under His protective hand. When our parents were going through too much to "be parents," God faithfully sent precious, dear, faithful friends into our lives to be spiritual mothers and fathers to us. They came in the form of pastors and lifelong friends who knew exactly what was happening at home, as well as new friends who had no idea.

Though it was the darkest season of my life, I am now able to look back and see how, through the process, God taught me to trust Him more. Because of all of the physical things breaking down around us, as well as the prayers from many friends and family, my brother and I both came to a place in which we were able to press into God deeply. We saw that His purposes for us didn't end with our parents' divorce. He still had plans to use us and to use our story, and He was still for us.

I love how God's faithfulness was proven when He provided this precious girl with a family. Nobody will ever be able to replace your parents, and that's not what God desires. But He faithfully adds people to your life if your parents are going through too much to be parents. Hold on to that promise from God. Open your eyes to see whom He has placed in your life.

Let Your Love Shine

"You are the light of the world—like a city on a hilltop that cannot be hidden. No one lights a lamp and then puts it under a basket. Instead, a lamp is placed on a stand, where it gives light to everyone in the house. In the same way, let your good deeds shine out for all to see, so that everyone will praise your heavenly Father" (Matthew 5:14-16 NLT). You are a light to the world. You are a light to your family—your mom, dad and siblings. You are a light to your household.

Did you notice that Matthew 5:15 says that when your light is placed on a lamp stand, it gives light to everyone in the house?

Loving your family means letting your light shine before them. Through serving them, you shine a light that will cause them to glorify your Father in Heaven. Ask the Lord what you can do to bless your family. If you listen, He will show you. "Or do you show contempt for the riches of his kindness, forbearance and patience, not realizing that God's kindness is intended to lead you to repentance?" (Romans 2:4 NIV). God's kindness leads people to change their ways. The love of God, displayed through your life and actions will be the light that your enemies are drawn toward.

Time to Love and to Pray

One of the most powerful and life-changing things you can do is to ask the Lord to search your heart and point out if there is anything that offends Him. Let's take a moment and ask the Lord to thoroughly search the depths of our hearts (Psalm 139:1). Is there a relationship that needs healing in your life? Is there an area of resentment that you need to deal with? Through God's great grace, you can take care of that right now. Pray this with me:

Dear Heavenly Father, I thank You for Your great grace. I believe that You have empowered me to do what the Bible says. Right now, I pray for _____. Father God, I know that You love them. And I believe with all my heart You want me to also love them with the same love that You have. So I make this commitment to love them as You do. Please show me how I can bless them and show them who You are. Thank You for helping me. In Jesus' name, amen.

Now, any time a negative thought comes up in your mind toward this person, what should you do? Pray for them. Bless them with your words and your life. That is how you overcome. After you pray, expect to see a change in them. Have faith in God and in what He can do. There are exciting days ahead of you. Trust God because when you do, you always win!

CHAPTER 8

THE BRAND NEW DAY

Overcoming Changes with Stepparents and New Siblings

If your parents have divorced or separated, things have probably changed in your life. Some of these changes may have been expected, while others were unexpected.

One of these changes may have been that your mom or dad got married again. Did this happen to you? _____

One of these changes may have been that you now have brothers and/or sisters you didn't have before. Did this happen to you? _____

If neither of these things happened in your life, they could someday. If they do, things will definitely be different. How do I know? This happened to me. Let me encourage you from my own experience. You don't have to be scared of the "new." You can trust God to take care of you and your new family. He will bring you to a place that is better than where you were before.

Your Life Is Being Rebuilt

"Once again I will build you up, and you will be rebuilt, my dear people Israel. Once again you will take your tambourines, and you will go dancing with happy people" (Jeremiah 31:4 GWT). Ecclesiastes 3 reminds us that "there is a time to build." Right now, you are in a season of being rebuilt. Your life is being reconstructed. This is a new day. Your life isn't how life used to be, but now can be even better. God is building you up. Once again, you can be joyful!

Everything is put into a new perspective when you realize *you're* the one God is working on. Isaiah 54:11-12 gives us a picture of this, "O storm-battered city, troubled and desolate! I will rebuild you with precious jewels and make your foundations from lapis lazuli. I will make your towers of sparkling rubies, your gates of shining gems, and your walls of precious stones" (NLT). I think it is interesting that God specifically mentioned the rebuilding of walls and gates. In the days in which this verse was written, both walls and gates were built to prevent the enemy from invading a city. Do you remember the walls of Jericho? When the walls fell down, the Israelites conquered the land.

As the Lord rebuilds your life, He rebuilds your defenses. You have been hurt, but He reconstructs the protective walls that have been torn down. The destruction that you have previously experienced in your life will no longer be there. God will put up walls to protect you from the enemy.

Now, read Jeremiah 31:4 and Isaiah 58:11-12 again, this time putting your name in the blanks.

"Once again I will build you up, and you will be rebuilt, my dear _____. Once again you will take your tambourines, and you will go dancing with happy people. O _____, storm-battered [one], troubled and desolate! I will rebuild you with precious jewels and make your foundations from lapis lazuli. I will make your towers of sparkling rubies, your gates of shining gems, and your walls of precious stones." God is the rebuilder of your life. He is the rebuilder of your relationships. Get ready to watch something beautiful take shape!

The New Thing

"Whoever is a believer in Christ is a new creation. The old way of living has disappeared. A new way of living has come into existence" (2 Corinthians 5:17 GWT). Once your parents separated or divorced, you were forced into a new way of life. As you recognize that these old things and old ways of doing things have passed away, your eyes will be open to see the new things Jesus is bringing into your life. He has a new beginning for you!

Your stepmom or stepdad will most likely be different than your biological mom or dad. When your new siblings come into your family, they might not feel like they "fit." The truth is they wouldn't have fit in the old plan you used to have for your life. But remember, God is doing a *new* thing. "Forget about what's happened; don't keep going over old history. Be alert, be present. I'm about to do something brand-new" (Isaiah 43:19 MSG).

When I met my stepdad, Steve, I wasn't accepting of him because his presence in my life made it different than before. I had to allow the Lord to work on my heart and show me what could happen if I opened up my heart to learn from him. So I did. Then, instead of seeing things that I thought were wrong about Steve, I started seeing things that were right about him—the positive things. And guess what? Once I started doing that, I realized the things I once thought were so negative actually turned out to be positive!

It wasn't because Steve changed. It was because my heart changed *toward* him. Today, I love the relationship we have. I learn so much from him and respect who he is. I am so thankful that he is in my life. Sure, my life is different now, but it's better because he is in it. If things were a little rough for you and your stepparent at first, don't let that affect what God has for you in the future. This new way of life is certainly an adjustment but with the Lord's help and wisdom, it can be a beautiful change. Trust me!

Instead of disliking or rejecting your new family members, focus on what you can learn from them. If you have the perspective that you can learn from someone new in your life, it will cause you to receive and embrace these new family members more freely. It will help you in your journey to love them as well.

If it is God's plan for them to come into your family, then He placed them there for a reason. It's up to you to discover that reason. God's plan is higher than your plan and His ways are higher than your ways. So always have an open heart and let what God wants to do come to pass in your life. These three "L's" will help you embrace your new family members: *Love* them, *listen* to what they have to say, and *learn* from them.

Have you had any challenges with your new family members?

_____

List some challenges you have experienced:

_____

_____

_____

_____

What effort can you make to help your new family members feel more accepted?

_____

_____

_____

_____

List some things you have learned from your stepmom, stepdad or siblings:

_____

_____

_____

_____

List at least ten things that you admire and respect about your stepmom or stepdad:

1. _____

2. _____

3. _____

4. _____

5. _____

6. _____

7. _____

8. _____

9. _____

10. _____

If this applies to you, list at least ten things you admire and love about your stepsisters and/or stepbrothers:

1. _____

2. _____

3. _____

4. _____

5. _____

6. _____

7. _____

8. _____

9. _____

10. _____

Let the Journey Continue

Wow, what a journey this has been. Together, we started out at a place of hurt and arrived at a place of love, forgiveness, and redemption that only God can bring us to through His grace. The journey is far from over, but now, as you face challenges, you know how to stand your ground. You understand that God promises you victory, but it is up to you to continually walk in faith when you don't see the victory yet. "For whatever is born of God is victorious over the world; and this is the victory that conquers the world, even our faith" (1 John 5:4 AMP).

In my life story, every relationship that was broken has been restored and made even better than it was before. Every "new" family member has taught me important life lessons, and I genuinely love them so dearly. This is a work that only God can do. He has truly done a new thing in my life, and I believe He will also do this in yours. God will continue to bring restoration to your relationships as you trust in Him.

As you continue on your journey, always remember that you have the Holy Spirit as your comforter. No matter what you face, He is always there. If you find yourself in a situation that is not addressed in this book, rely on Him for direction. Listen to the Spirit of God and He will guide you. "When the Friend comes, the Spirit of the Truth, he will take you by the hand and guide you into all the truth there is. He won't draw attention to himself, but will make sense out of what is about to happen and, indeed, out of all that I have done and said" (John 16:13 MSG).

You are more than a conqueror through our Lord Jesus Christ. You are the son or daughter of an ever-present Father. His approach toward you is love. His thoughts toward you are peace. You're not a statistic. You have a powerful testimony—*you have a Father and He loves you!*

What Does God Say About You?

❖ **You are special.**

"O LORD you have examined my heart and know everything about me. You know when I sit down or stand up. You know my thoughts even when I'm far away. You see me when I travel and when I rest at home. You know everything I do. You know what I am going to say even before I say it, LORD. You go before me and follow me. You place your hand of blessing on my head. Such knowledge is too wonderful for me, too great for me to understand! I can never escape from your Spirit! I can never get away from your presence. You made all the delicate, inner parts of my body and knit me together in my mother's womb. Thank you for making me so wonderfully complex! Your workmanship is marvelous—how well I know it. You watched me as I was being formed in utter seclusion, as I was woven together in the dark of the womb. You saw me before I was born. Every day of my life was recorded in your book. Every moment was laid out before a single day had passed. How precious are your thoughts about me, O God. They cannot be numbered! I can't even count them; they outnumber the grains of sand! And when I wake up, you are still with me!"

(Psalm 139:1-7, 13-18 NLT)

❖ **I love you forever.**

"The LORD has appeared of old to me, saying: 'Yes, I have loved you with an everlasting love; Therefore with lovingkindness I have drawn you.'"

(Jeremiah 31:3 NKJV)

❖ **My Son Jesus died for you so that I could be your Daddy. You are my child!**

"This resurrection life you received from God is not a timid, grave-tending life. It's adventurously expectant, greeting God with a childlike 'What's next, Papa?' God's Spirit touches our spirits and confirms who we really are. We know who he is, and we know who we are: Father and children. And we know we are going to get what's coming to us—an unbelievable inheritance! We go through exactly what Christ goes through. If we go through the hard times with him, then we're certainly going to go through the good times with him!"

(Romans 8:15-17 MSG)

❖ **I have good plans for you and for your tomorrow.**

"'For I know the plans I have for you,' says the LORD. 'They are plans for good and not for disaster, to give you a future and a hope.'"

(Jeremiah 29:11 NLT)

❖ **Don't worry about anything. Just talk to Me and I'll take care of it.**

"Give all your worries and cares to God, for he cares about you."

(1 Peter 5:7 NLT)

❖ **I am your friend! I love to talk to you and spend time with you.**

"I no longer call you slaves, because a master doesn't confide in his slaves. Now you are my friends, since I have told you everything the Father told me."

(John 15:15 NLT)

❖ **I like it when you come to Me. I'll never tell you to go away.**

"But Jesus said, 'Let the children come to me. Don't stop them! For the Kingdom of Heaven belongs to those who are like these children.'"

(Matthew 19:14 NLT)

❖ **I will never, EVER leave you.**

"*Let* your conduct be without covetousness; be content with such things as you have. For He Himself has said, 'I will never leave you nor forsake you.'"

(Hebrews 13:5 NKJV)

❖ **You are going to make it. In Me, you always win!**

"And who can win this battle against the world? Only those who believe that Jesus is the Son of God."

(1 John 5:5 NLT)

❖ **I came to heal your broken heart.**

"The Spirit of the LORD *is* upon Me, because He has anointed Me to preach the gospel to the poor; He has sent Me to heal the brokenhearted, to proclaim liberty to the captives and recovery of sight to the blind, to set at liberty those who are oppressed."

(Luke 4:18 NKJV)

ENDNOTES

1 Frank F. Furstenberg, Jr., Christine Winquist Nord, James L. Peterson, Nicholas Zill, "The Life Course of Children of Divorce: Martial Disruption and Parental Contact," *American Sociological Review*, Vol. 48 No. 5 (October 1983): http://www.jstor.org/disco ver/10.2307/2094925?uid=3739848&uid=2129&uid=2&uid=70 &uid=4&uid=3739256&sid=21102564150373.

2 Wade F. Horn and Andrew S. Bush, *Fathers, Marriage and Welfare Reform* (Washington, DC: Hudson Institute, 1997).

3 Nicholas Wolfinger, *Understanding the Divorce Cycle: The Children of Divorce in their Own Marriages* (Cambridge UK: Cambridge University Press, 2005).

4 John H. Tripp and Monica Cockett, "Parents, parenting, and family breakdown," *Archives of Disease in Childhood*, Vol. 78 Issue 2 (1998): http://adc.bmj.com/content/78/2/104.full.

5 Nan Marie Astone and Sara S. McLanahan, "Family Structure, Parental Practices and High School Completion," *Amercian Sociological Review*, Vol. 56 (1991): 309-320.

6 Robert L. Flewelling and Karl E. Bauman, "Family Structure as a Predictor of Initial Substance Use and Sexual Intercourse in Early Adolescence," *Journal of Marriage and the Family,* Vol. 52 (1990): 171-181.

7 University of Hawaii, "Estimate the Number of Grains of Sand on all the Beaches of the Earth", *21st Century Problem Solving:* http://www.hawaii.edu/suremath/jsand.html (accessed 9-19-2013).

NOTES

NOTES

NOTES

ABOUT THE AUTHOR

Jenny Kutz, minister and author, has been a part of ministry for as long as she can remember. She started preaching in children's church at the age of 12 years old and has continued to minister ever since. She attended Oral Roberts University in Tulsa, OK in 2005 and studied Worship Leadership and Pastoral Ministry with an emphasis on youth.

As the granddaughter of well-known ministers, Kenneth and Gloria Copeland, Jenny has seen faith and love lived out in a real way. She has had hands on training in ministry through various mission outreaches, serving in the local church and assisting her grandparents as they ministered.

Jenny has faith to see this generation rise up and live out the great commission. Her heart is to see the gospel of Jesus Christ spread to the nations. Out of that desire, Jenny began Love to the Nations, a ministry dedicated to share the Love of God to people who have never heard.

She also founded Global Girls Bible Study, an online Bible study for women from all around the world. You can watch the Bible Studies online at www.globalgirlsbiblestudy. com.

Jenny makes her home in Fort Worth, TX.

The Harrison House Vision

Proclaiming the truth and the power
Of the Gospel of Jesus Christ
With excellence;

Challenging Christians to
Live victoriously,
Grow spiritually,
Know God intimately.

Fast. Easy.
Convenient.

For the latest Harrison House product information and author news, look no further than your computer. All the details on our powerful, life-changing products are just a click away. New releases, E-mail subscriptions, testimonies, monthly specials—find it all in one place. Visit harrisonhouse.com today!

harrisonhouse

PRAYER OF SALVATION

God loves you—no matter who you are, no matter what your past. God loves you so much that He gave His one and only begotten Son for you. The Bible tells us that "...whoever believes in Him shall not perish but have eternal life" (John 3:16 NIV). Jesus laid down His life and rose again so that we could spend eternity with Him in heaven and experience His absolute best on earth. If you would like to receive Jesus into your life, say the following prayer out loud and mean it from your heart.

Heavenly Father, I come to You admitting that I am a sinner. Right now, I choose to turn away from sin, and I ask You to cleanse me of all unrighteousness. I believe that Your Son, Jesus, died on the cross to take away my sins. I also believe that He rose again from the dead so that I might be forgiven of my sins and made righteous through faith in Him. I call upon the name of Jesus Christ to be the Savior and Lord of my life. Jesus, I choose to follow You and ask that You fill me with the power of the Holy Spirit. I declare that right now I am a child of God. I am free from sin and full of the righteousness of God. I am saved in Jesus' name. Amen.

If you prayed this prayer to receive Jesus Christ as your Savior for the first time, please contact us on the Web at **www.harrisonhouse.com** to receive a free book.

Or you may write to us at
Harrison House • P.O. Box 35035 • Tulsa, Oklahoma 74153